BUILDING BLOCKS OF GEOGRAPHY

HUMAN GEOGRAPHY

Written by Alex Woolf

Illustrated by Emiliano Migliardo

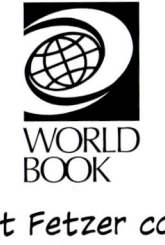

WORLD BOOK

a Scott Fetzer company
Chicago

World Book, Inc.
180 North LaSalle Street
Suite 900
Chicago, Illinois 60601
USA

For information about other World Book publications, visit our website at www.worldbook.com or call **1-800-WORLDBK (967-5325)**.
For information about sales to schools and libraries, call 1-800-975-3250 (United States), or 1-800-837-5365 (Canada).

© 2023 World Book, Inc. All rights reserved. This volume may not be reproduced in whole or in part in any form without prior written permission from the publisher.

WORLD BOOK and the GLOBE DEVICE are registered trademarks or trademarks of World Book, Inc.

Library of Congress Cataloging-in-Publication Data for this volume has been applied for.

Building Blocks of Geography
ISBN: 978-0-7166-4275-6 (set, hc.)

Human Geography
ISBN: 978-0-7166-4281-7 (hc.)

Also available as:
ISBN: 978-0-7166-4291-6 (e-book)

Printed in India by Thomson Press (India) Limited, Uttar Pradesh, India
1st printing June 2022

WORLD BOOK STAFF
Executive Committee
President: Geoff Broderick
Vice President, Editorial: Tom Evans
Vice President, Finance: Donald D. Keller
Vice President, Marketing: Jean Lin
Vice President, International: Eddy Kisman
Vice President, Technology: Jason Dole
Director, Human Resources: Bev Ecker

Editorial
Manager, New Content: Jeff De La Rosa
Associate Manager, New Product: Nicholas Kilzer
Sr. Editor: Shawn Brennan
Proofreader: Nathalie Strassheim

Graphics and Design
Sr. Visual Communications Designer: Melanie Bender
Coordinator, Design Development: Brenda Tropinski
Sr. Web Designer/Digital Media Developer: Matt Carrington

Acknowledgments:
Writer: Alex Woolf
Illustrator: Emiliano Migliardo
Series advisor: Marjorie Frank

Developed with World Book by White-Thomson Publishing LTD
www.wtpub.co.uk

TABLE OF CONTENTS

Humans on Earth 4
Where Humans Live 6
Landscape 8
Farming and Fishing.......................10
Natural Resources 12
Energy 14
Transportation 16
Tourism and Recreation 18
Challenges 20
Modifying the Environment 24
Technology 28
Bad Impacts 30
Making Things Better 34
Can You Believe It?! 38
Words to Know 40

There is a glossary on page 40. Terms defined in the glossary are in type **that looks like this** on their first appearance.

HUMANS ON EARTH

Hi there! I'm Earth. I don't want to brag, but I'm a remarkably diverse planet.

I have warm parts...

...and cold parts. Brrr!

Tropical forests...

...and arid deserts. Some water would be nice!

4

Hey, this is fun! I have hills and valleys...
...rivers and seas.
Humans have found ways to live in all these different **environments** and adapt to them.
In this book you'll see how human societies have been shaped by the geography of where they live.
You'll also discover how humans have made a big impact on their environment, and this is often quite damaging.
Humans need to try and look after their planet.
After all, there's only one of me!

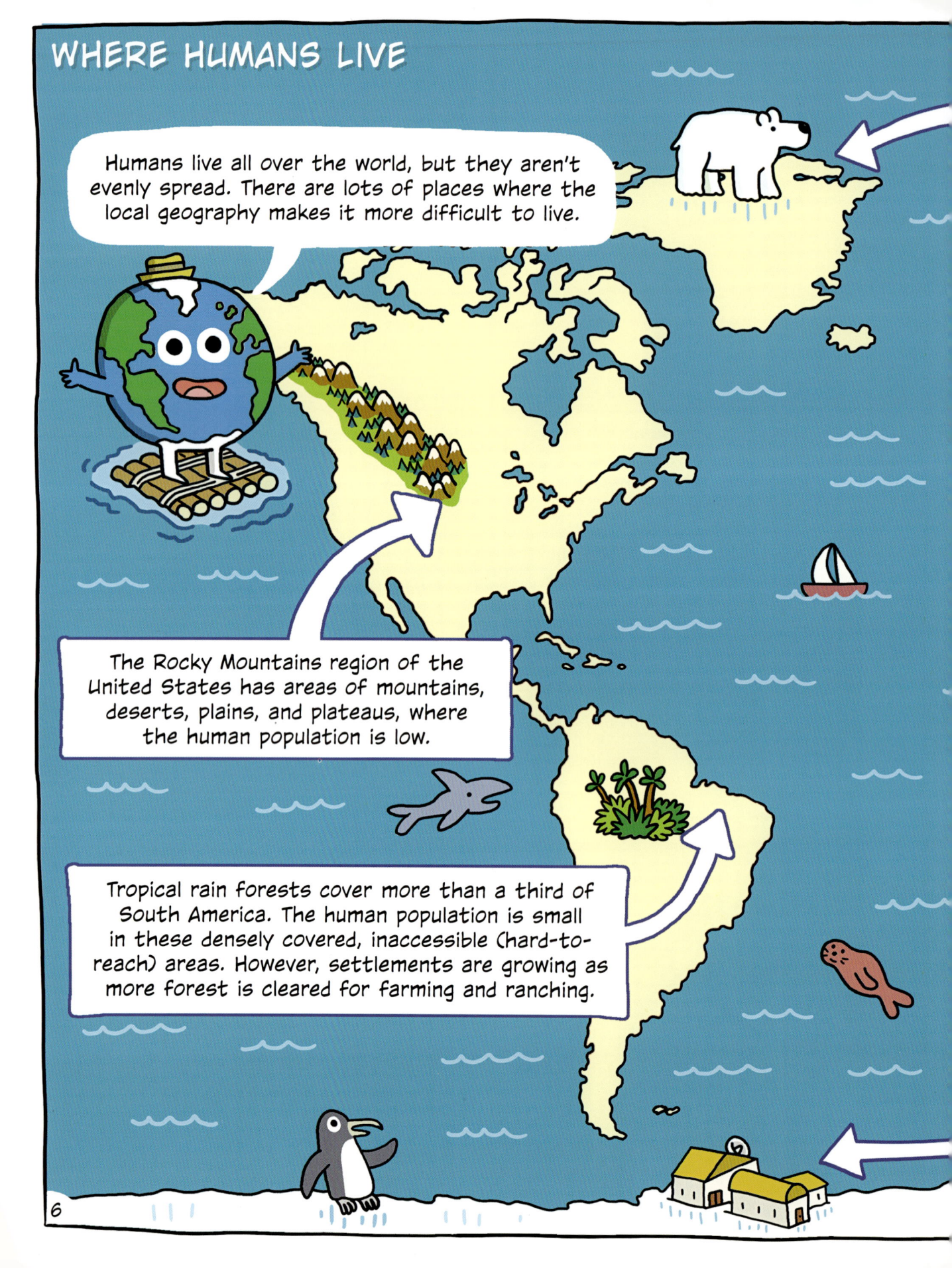

WHERE HUMANS LIVE

Humans live all over the world, but they aren't evenly spread. There are lots of places where the local geography makes it more difficult to live.

The Rocky Mountains region of the United States has areas of mountains, deserts, plains, and plateaus, where the human population is low.

Tropical rain forests cover more than a third of South America. The human population is small in these densely covered, inaccessible (hard-to-reach) areas. However, settlements are growing as more forest is cleared for farming and ranching.

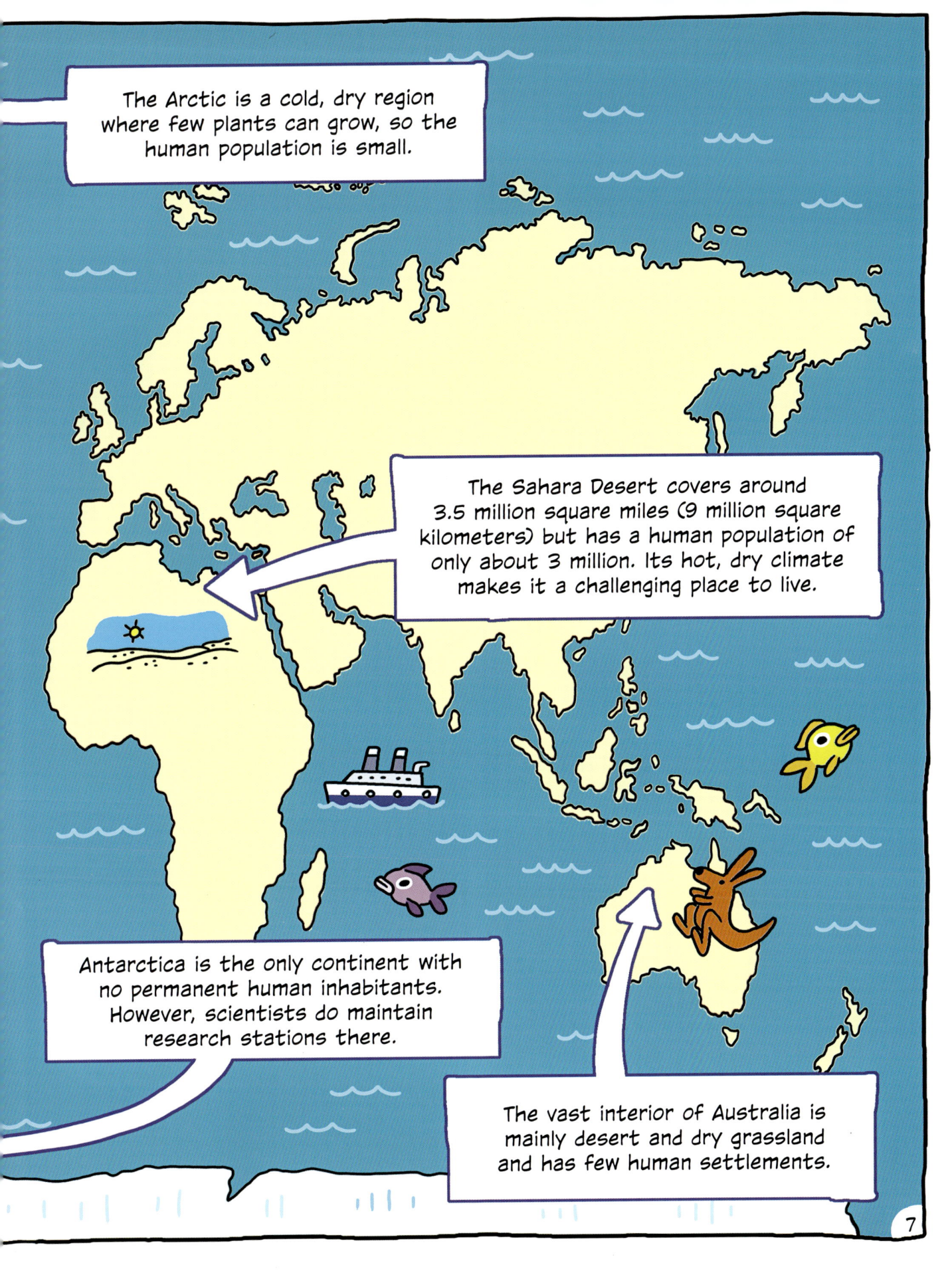

The Arctic is a cold, dry region where few plants can grow, so the human population is small.

The Sahara Desert covers around 3.5 million square miles (9 million square kilometers) but has a human population of only about 3 million. Its hot, dry climate makes it a challenging place to live.

Antarctica is the only continent with no permanent human inhabitants. However, scientists do maintain research stations there.

The vast interior of Australia is mainly desert and dry grassland and has few human settlements.

LANDSCAPE

When looking for a place to settle, humans need to consider the **topography** (natural features) of the land.

Flat land can give you lots of space for buildings, but it can be a bit windy... *I said it can be a bit windy!*

A location with natural shelter from the elements can be great...

...so long as you have enough space to build!

Building on a flat site is ideal. Slopes can offer more of a challenge.

Back in olden times, a high place was often a good place to build a castle, because it was easier to defend... I see you!

People still choose to live on top of hills today, although not usually for defense. It might be a slog getting up there...

...but the views can be spectacular!

FARMING AND FISHING

The human need for food has had an enormous impact on Earth's geography, although this wasn't always the case...

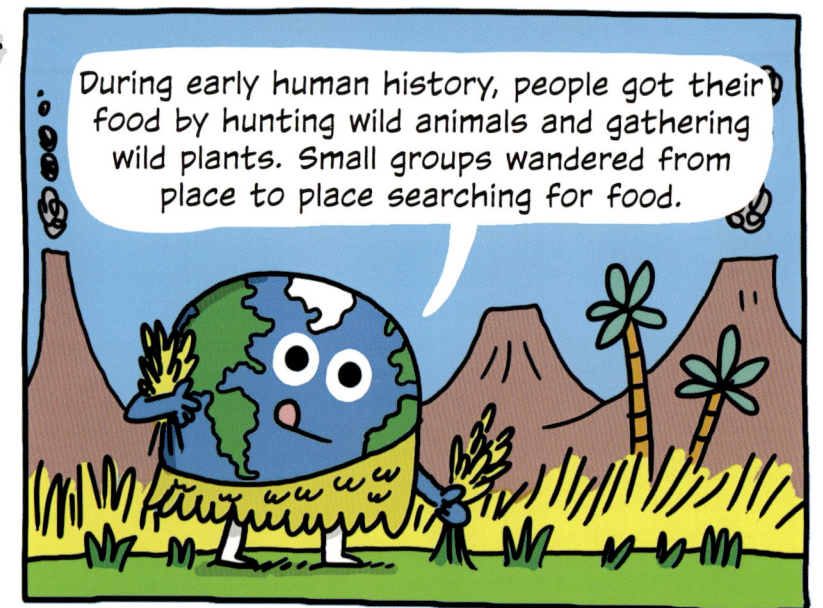

During early human history, people got their food by hunting wild animals and gathering wild plants. Small groups wandered from place to place searching for food.

There was no reason to settle down in one place. But this lifestyle had its challenges... Help!

Around 10,000 years ago, humans developed **agriculture.** People began to settle where there was fertile soil and enough water for growing crops.

Early people settled in fertile river valleys, such as the Nile Valley, where Egypt is today.

Nice wig!

Today, thanks to modern technology and better transport links, people no longer need to live near where food is produced. Now most people live in cities.

Wow! This is so much easier than hunting and gathering!

Today, farms cover around 40 percent of Earth's land surface. Many farms grow single crops on enormous fields. They have transformed the landscape.

Ranchers raise cattle or sheep on huge farms in flat, open grassland.

Coastal communities harvest fish from the sea. Fishing crews go out to sea in **trawlers** and catch the fish in large nets. Other people in the port process the catch and sell it.

NATURAL RESOURCES

Humans have always made use of Earth's **natural resources**. Natural resources are raw materials occurring in nature that can be used by humans.

Some of these resources are found on the surface, like trees, which we use for timber, or for burning as fuel.

Or like clean water for drinking and washing, which can be collected from a stream. So refreshing!

Other resources are found beneath the ground. People dig wells to reach groundwater—water that has collected beneath the soil.

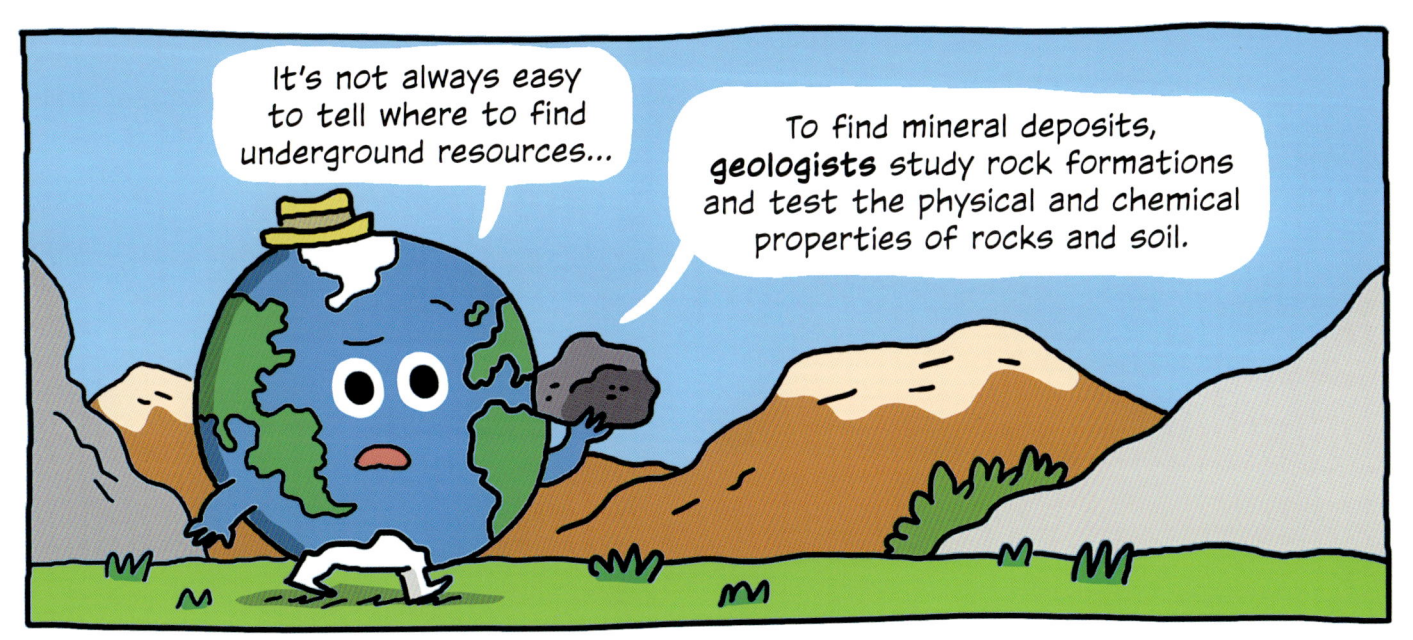

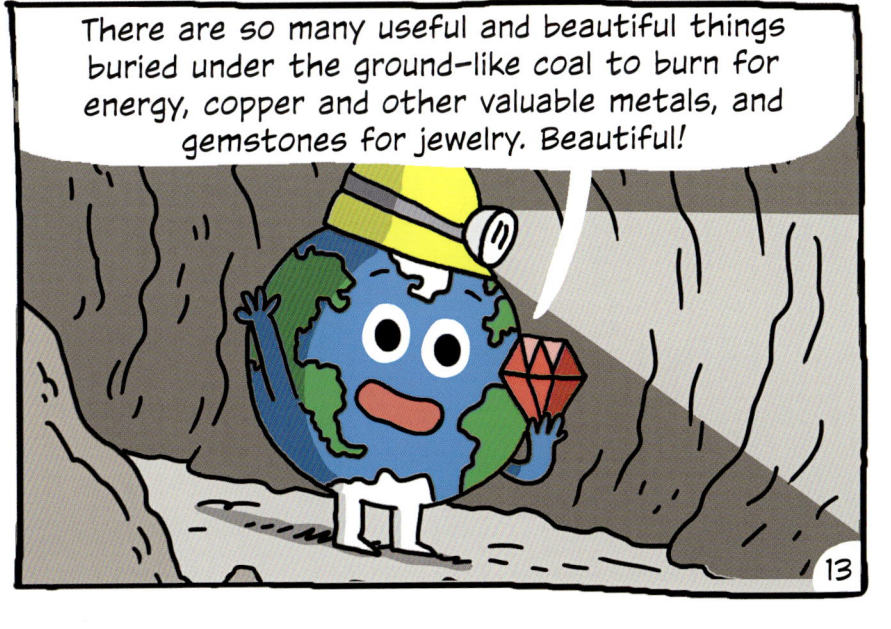

It's not always easy to tell where to find underground resources...

To find mineral deposits, **geologists** study rock formations and test the physical and chemical properties of rocks and soil.

Whoa, this is fun! Quarries are big holes dug in the ground from which rocks and minerals are extracted. Gravel, sand, limestone, and copper are obtained this way.

Hey, it's dark around here! To obtain materials such as iron **ore** or gold, shafts are dug deep into the Earth to reach the materials. These are called shaft mines.

There are so many useful and beautiful things buried under the ground—like coal to burn for energy, copper and other valuable metals, and gemstones for jewelry. Beautiful!

ENERGY

"This is my friend **Energy**!"

"Humans need energy for their vehicles, machines, homes, and workplaces. They need it for warmth and to cook with."

For centuries, people have mined or drilled for **fossil fuels** to provide for their energy needs. These are fuels made from ancient plants and animals buried long ago.

"Fossil fuels are coal, crude oil, and natural gas, found in deposits deep underground."

When fossil fuels are burned, they emit carbon dioxide, which traps the sun's heat in the atmosphere, adding to global warming.

"They're also nonrenewable—they'll eventually run out, or become too expensive to extract."

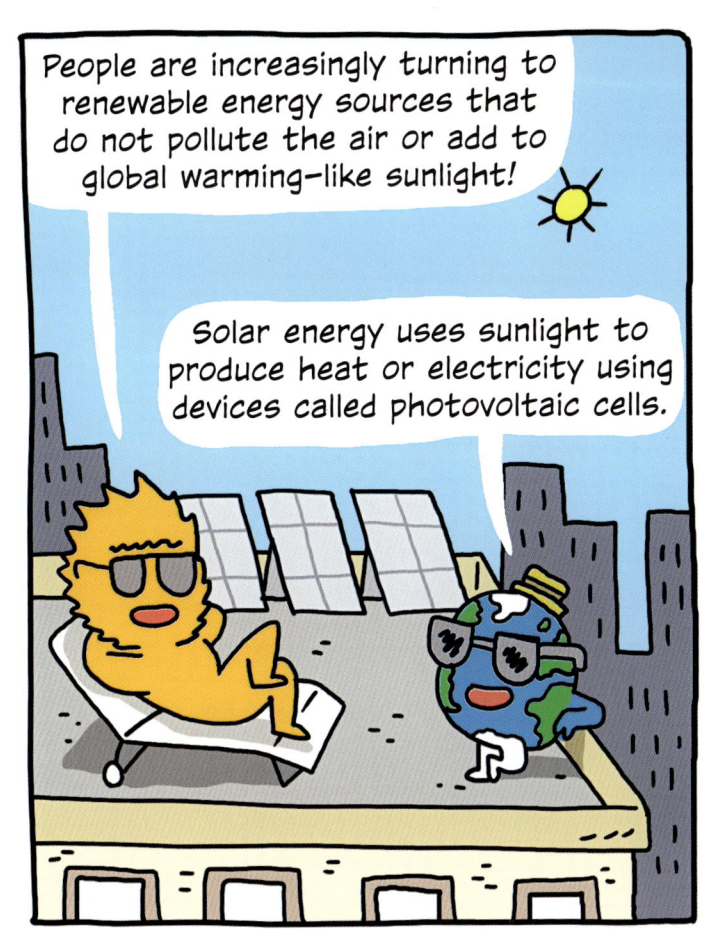

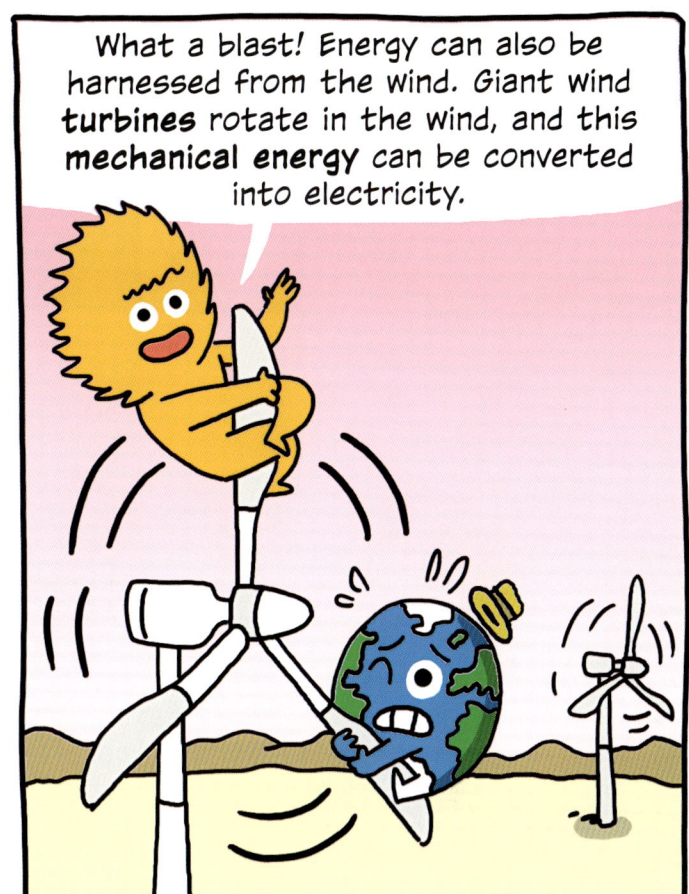

People are increasingly turning to renewable energy sources that do not pollute the air or add to global warming—like sunlight!

Solar energy uses sunlight to produce heat or electricity using devices called photovoltaic cells.

What a blast! Energy can also be harnessed from the wind. Giant wind **turbines** rotate in the wind, and this **mechanical energy** can be converted into electricity.

Gurgle... Flowing water is another source of renewable energy, harnessed by watermills and **hydroelectric power** plants.

Whoa! Hot stuff! There are vast stores of heat energy beneath Earth's surface. We see glimpses of it with volcanoes. Geothermal energy, as it's called, can be used to heat buildings.

I'm outta here!

TRANSPORTATION

People will always need to move about—for school, work, or pleasure. So the places where humans settle need good transportation links.

Many towns and cities were built next to rivers because people can sail boats and ships along them to reach other places.

Rivers are like natural highways, but they don't always take people where they want to go. Hey, I want to turn left here...

MOTEL

That's why roads are needed. Roads have had a huge impact on the landscape. Along with the roads came gas stations, motels, restaurants, and shops.

Railroads are tracks on which trains run. Trains take passengers and **freight** over long distances, often at very fast speeds.

As railroads spread across continents, builders constructed stations where passengers could stop or switch trains. Some of these rail hubs grew from small towns into huge cities.

An even faster way of transporting passengers and freight is by airplane. Whee!

Airplanes land and take off from airports. They need a lot of land for runways, hangars, parking lots, and terminals.

The largest airports can be the size of a town. I could live here!

It's amazing how the human desire and need to travel has had such an impact on the physical environment.

TOURISM AND RECREATION

I have to admit, I can be beautiful in places...

Humans are naturally attracted to my most scenic spots, such as lakes and beaches...

...or forests and flower-filled meadows.

They like to go to places with opportunities for fun and outdoor activities.

But these aren't always practical places to live all year round. There aren't enough jobs to support a big population.

The activities are often seasonal. Warm weather isn't great for skiing...

...and cold weather isn't brilliant for swimming in lakes and rivers.

Besides, if everyone lived in these beautiful places, they might not stay beautiful for very long!

So people build resorts and hotels in places of natural beauty to attract seasonal tourists.

CHALLENGES

"So far we've looked at many ways that humans make use of their local geography."

"But geography often places limits on human activity."

"For example, the shape of the landscape where someone lives can be challenging."

"For those living on hills and mountains, building is difficult and expensive, because land first has to be made level."

"Roads can be steep, twisty, and sometimes dangerous to drive on."

20

People living on small islands can feel cut off. Getting supplies can take longer. Now where is that ship?

People living in valleys, near rivers, or by the sea are at risk of flooding from storms.

In hot, arid climates, a **drought** can cause crops to fail and water sources to dry up.

In cold regions, roads often get blocked in winter due to snow or become hazardous because of ice.

Sometimes, nature can unleash destructive forces that can threaten people's homes, jobs, and lives.

Hello, I'm over here! The weather can often turn dangerous. Blizzards are heavy, blinding snowstorms that occur in cold climates.

Hurricanes are violent, whirling storms that form over warm ocean waters. When they strike land, they whip up the sea into huge waves called storm surges that can cause major flooding.

A volcano is an opening in Earth's crust. Molten (melted) rock may be forced up from underground and erupt onto the surface.

Volcanoes can destroy homes and communities with flows of lava, red-hot ash, and gas, or mud. Help!

Millions of people live in places at risk from volcanoes. Many choose to live there because volcanoes produce fertile soil, which is good to farm.

Earthquakes occur along the boundaries of Earth's **tectonic plates**. Movement of the plates puts pressure on the rocks at these boundaries.

The breaking of the rocks releases waves of energy through the ground. This causes the earth to shake and buildings and other structures to collapse.

An undersea volcano or earthquake may cause a tsunami—a powerful ocean wave that can destroy coastal communities.

MODIFYING THE ENVIRONMENT

Over the centuries, humans have found ingenious ways of modifying their environment to overcome the challenges of local geography.

Road-builders often build bridges to get over such natural obstacles as rivers, lakes, and canyons. With most bridges, the weight is supported by a *pier* like this.

Suspension bridges span great distances over deep water or canyons, where piers are difficult to build. Steel cables and towers bear the bridge's weight.

No pier here, see!

If you can't go round or over it, go through it! Sometimes the best solution for road-builders is to dig a tunnel through a hill or mountain.

Farmers living in hilly areas can increase the amount of land they use to grow crops by building **terraces** into the slopes.

People living in some flood-prone areas build houses raised on stilts. Any room for me up there?

Those living in storm-prone areas build dome-shaped homes. The curved shape is better at withstanding high winds. Whee! This is fun!

In earthquake zones, architects design buildings to give them strong yet flexible frameworks. This way, the buildings sway rather than collapse in an earthquake.

Humans have always modified their local geography to get the resources they need from land and water.

Cough! Splutter! Farmers plow the soil to prepare it for planting. The plow loosens and turns over the soil, bringing fresh nutrients to the surface.

Some people clear forests to make room for farmland.

If the sea erodes a beach, people dredge (scoop out) sand from inland or offshore to rebuild it.

People dam rivers to create an artificial lake or reservoir. Sorry, river, I need your water!

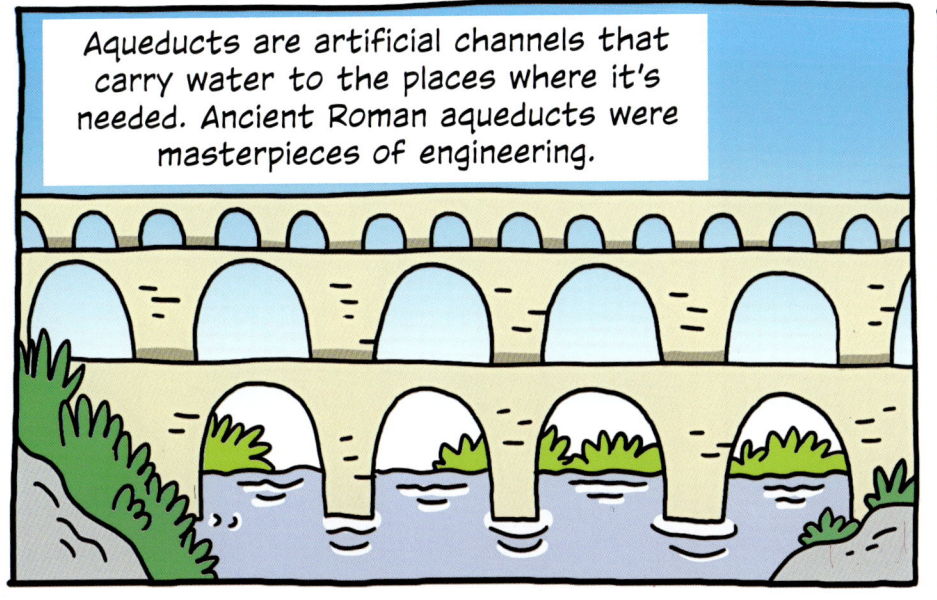

Some farmers build dams to divert rivers from their natural course so they can irrigate their fields.

And for my next trick, I will create land from the sea! Sometimes people reclaim land from oceans, lakes, and wetlands.

They do this by draining the water from the area and filling it with rock, clay, and soil. I need a break from this! How about a **canal** ride?

Canals are artificial waterways dug for transporting people and goods. What a delightful way to travel!

Aqueducts are artificial channels that carry water to the places where it's needed. Ancient Roman aqueducts were masterpieces of engineering.

There's really no end to the human desire to modify the natural environment! To see what I mean, try to imagine your neighborhood before humans arrived.

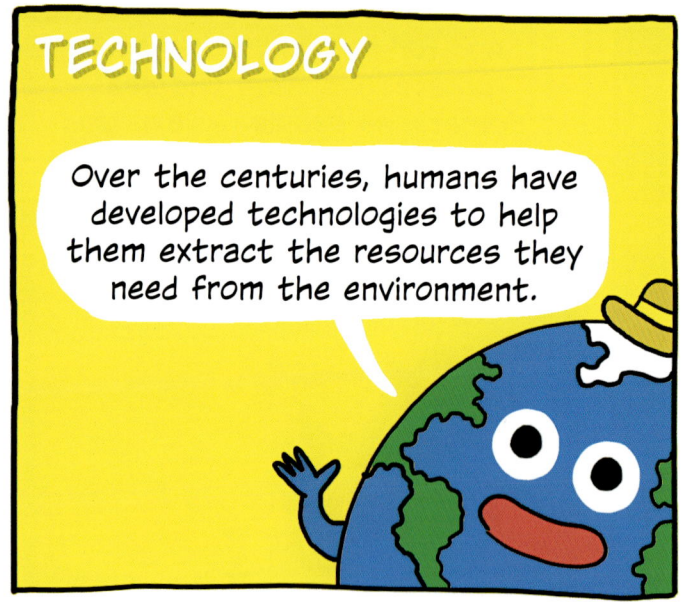

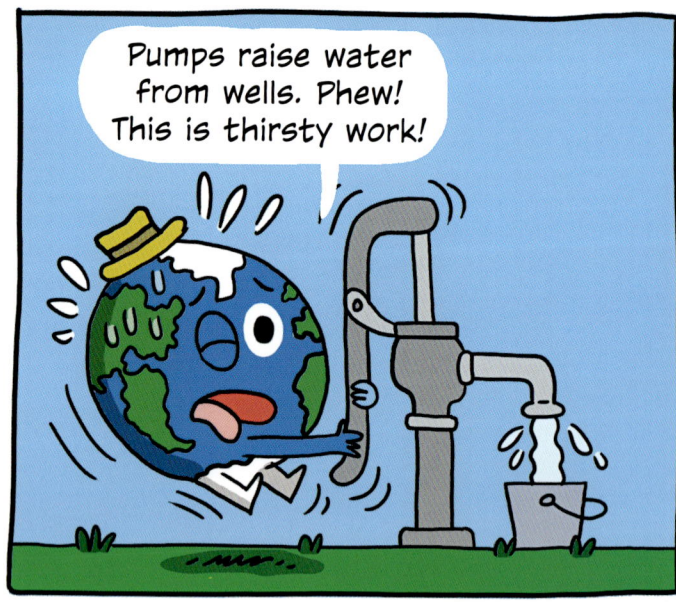

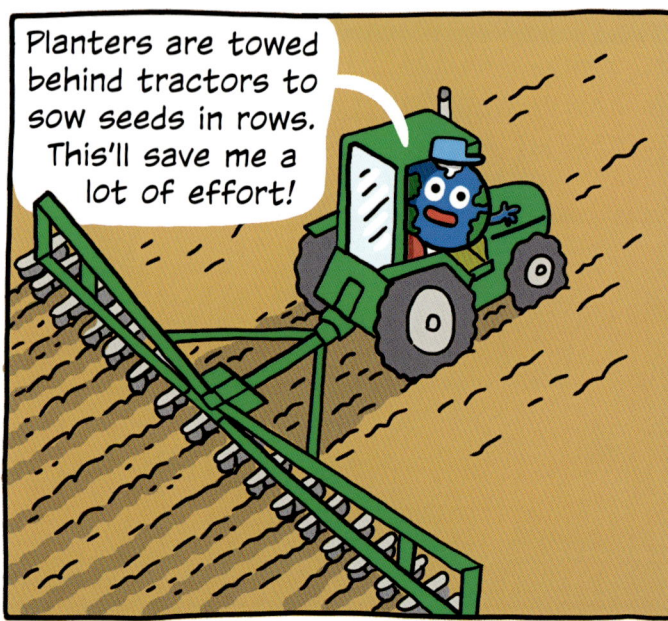

TECHNOLOGY

Over the centuries, humans have developed technologies to help them extract the resources they need from the environment.

Explosives are used to break up the rock in a quarry. Wow, that was loud!

Drills bore holes into mud and rock to reach oil reserves.

Pumps raise water from wells. Phew! This is thirsty work!

Filters remove impurities from water so it is safe for drinking.

FILTERED WATER

UNTREATED WATER

Planters are towed behind tractors to sow seeds in rows. This'll save me a lot of effort!

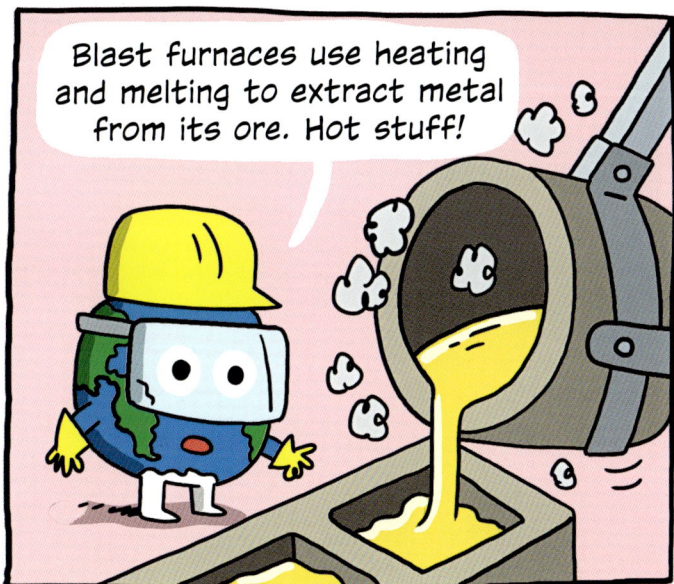

People also need technology to turn raw materials into products that can be sold.

Blast furnaces use heating and melting to extract metal from its ore. Hot stuff!

Automated machines in factories package goods. Dull work for humans. Luckily machines don't mind it!

The products humans make are bought and sold online, thanks to computer technology.

Computer technology and modern transportation ensure that people receive their purchases quickly—often the next day!

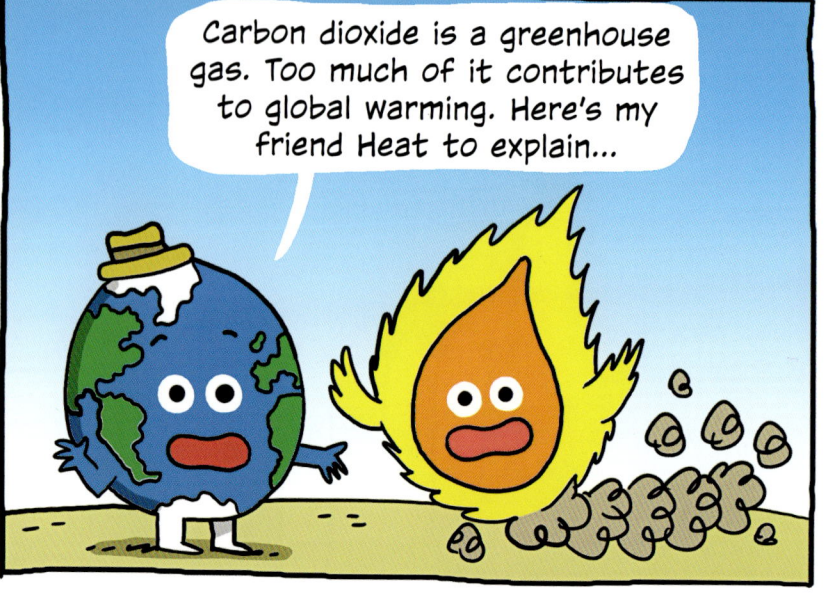

BAD IMPACTS

When humans modify their environment and extract resources, a lot of damage can be caused.

When forests are cleared to harvest timber or create farmland, the plant and animal species that lived there have nowhere to go. This reduces **biodiversity**.

Trees absorb the carbon dioxide gas that we breathe out and release the oxygen we need to live. Many human activities, such as burning fossil fuels, add extra carbon dioxide to the atmosphere.

CARBON DIOXIDE

OXYGEN

If trees are chopped down, they can no longer absorb carbon dioxide. Burning them adds carbon dioxide to the atmosphere.

Cough! Cough!

Carbon dioxide is a greenhouse gas. Too much of it contributes to global warming. Here's my friend Heat to explain...

If it weren't for the **"greenhouse effect,"** Earth would be a ball of ice. But gases such as water vapor, carbon dioxide, and methane naturally help to hold in some of the heat from the sun. They act like the glass in a giant greenhouse!

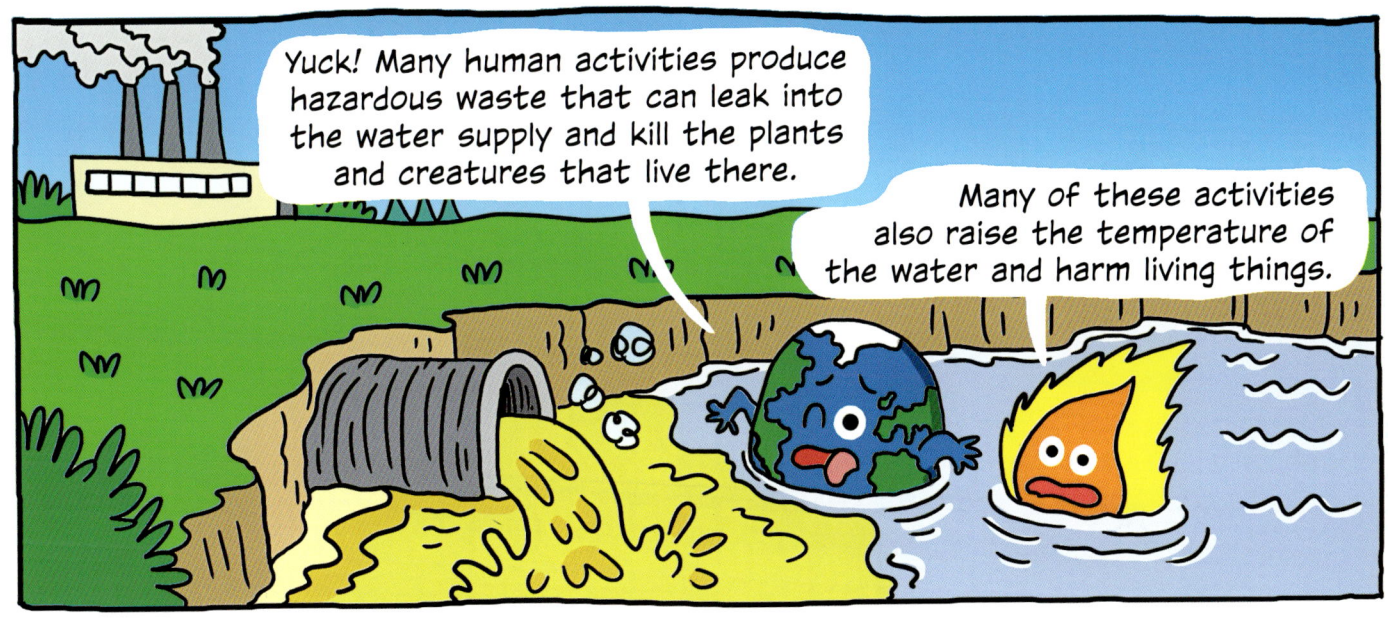

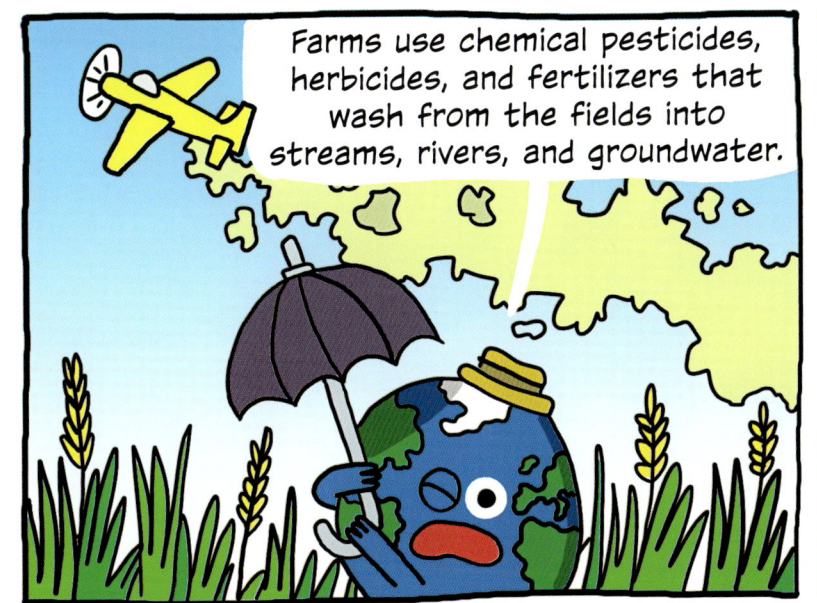

However, when too many of these gases get into the atmosphere, I get trapped in the atmosphere and Earth gets too warm.

Yuck! Many human activities produce hazardous waste that can leak into the water supply and kill the plants and creatures that live there.

Many of these activities also raise the temperature of the water and harm living things.

Farms use chemical pesticides, herbicides, and fertilizers that wash from the fields into streams, rivers, and groundwater.

When **mining** industries separate a mineral from its ore, the process generates a harmful waste called *tailings* that can end up polluting waterways.

IRON ORE

31

Power plants, paper mills, steelworks, and petroleum refineries are often built near lakes and rivers, which they use in their manufacturing processes. In some countries, factory waste often ends up being dumped in these bodies of water.

Nets used by fishing trawlers can also catch many other species, like dolphins and sea turtles.

Help, we're trapped!

The expansion of cities has caused a loss of wildlife habitat and an increase in pollution. You've got to stop, City!

But I want to grow!

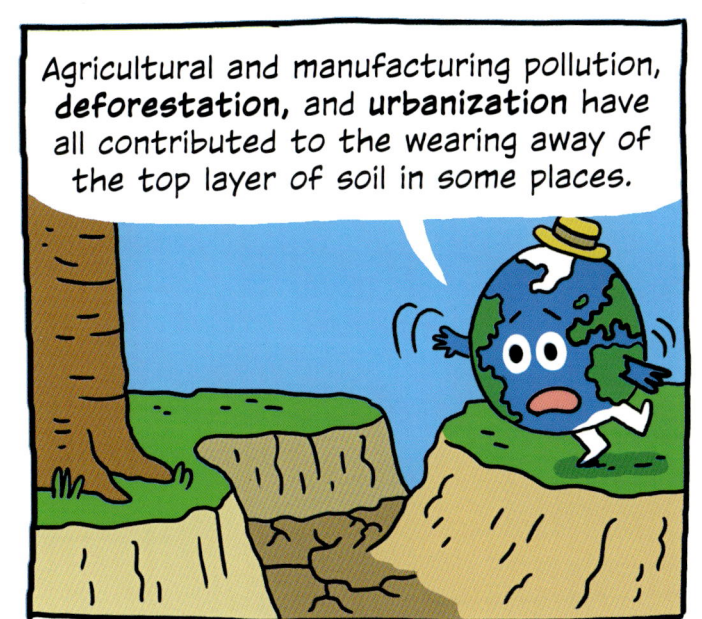

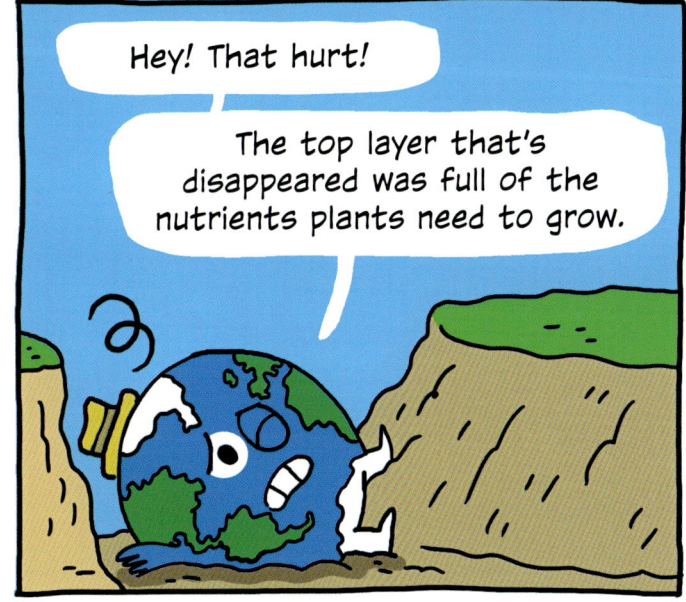

Panel 1: Agricultural and manufacturing pollution, **deforestation,** and **urbanization** have all contributed to the wearing away of the top layer of soil in some places.

Panel 2:
Hey! That hurt!

The top layer that's disappeared was full of the nutrients plants need to grow.

Panel 3: Soil erosion makes the land unfit for farming and can eventually turn it into desert. I feel parched!

Panel 4: By expanding our cities and destroying wildlife habitats, and by hunting or capturing animals, we've helped push thousands of plant and animal species to the brink of **extinction**.

Panel 5: The ivory-billed woodpecker of southeastern USA and Cuba has recently been declared likely extinct.

MAKING THINGS BETTER

By extracting what they need from the planet and modifying its geography, humans have made things better for themselves in many ways.

Expanding the amount of farmland, and farming it more intensively, has increased the food supply. In my day, meals were much smaller!

With improved transportation, food can be shipped all over the world, making diets more varied. Yum!

Technological advances in transportation have also greatly expanded travel opportunities.

34

Many of today's medicines were developed from substances found in nature, including plants, fungi, and bacteria. Now, what does this one do?

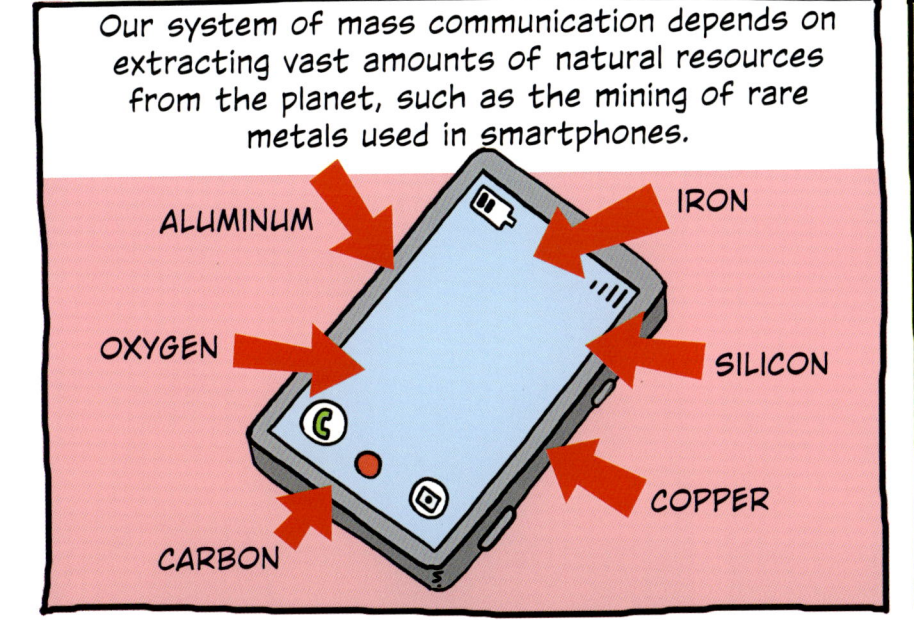

Creating these medicines has improved global health and life expectancy.

Will it taste nasty?

Modern **telecommunication** systems, including the cell phone network and the internet...

...allow instant global communication!

Our system of mass communication depends on extracting vast amounts of natural resources from the planet, such as the mining of rare metals used in smartphones.

ALUMINUM
IRON
OXYGEN
SILICON
COPPER
CARBON

Humans have certainly made the world more comfortable for themselves, but this has come at a cost to the planet. Are there ways of living that do less damage?

YES! There are ways! Today, many individuals, organizations, and governments are looking at ways to reduce the human impact on the planet and to improve the environment. There's a lot you can do to help.

Reduce, reuse, and recycle the things you use. The more we do this, the less need there is to harvest or extract more raw materials from Earth.

Shop wisely. Bring a reusable shopping bag, and buy local produce where possible.

Before buying seafood, check which species are relatively abundant. Avoid species that are overfished.

Help reduce greenhouse gas emissions by using energy-efficient light bulbs. And always switch lights off when you leave the room!

"Cycle and walk more. Drive less. This can be fun, and it's saving the planet!"

"Plant a tree. You, my friend, are absorbing carbon dioxide and providing us with oxygen."

"Doing my bit to combat global warming."

TAP TAP

"Volunteer for clean-ups in your community. It's fun, and you'll help make your local area more beautiful."

"Talk to others about the importance of protecting the planet."

"You'll make me very proud!"

37

CAN YOU BELIEVE IT?!

Earth scientists estimate that about **27,000 trees** are cut down every day just to make toilet paper!

The **Northern Hemisphere,** the half of Earth that is north of the equator, is home to almost 90 percent **of all people on Earth!**

Landscape

can change over time! The Sahara in northern Africa is the largest desert in the world. But 10,000 years ago, it was a rich grassland with abundant animals, plants, and even lakes!

Indonesia has the most **active volcanoes** of any country on Earth. At least 139 active volcanoes can be found there!

38

The Philippines consists of **more than 7,000 islands,** but only about **1,000 of them are inhabited.**

People developed **agriculture** independently in ancient times in several regions—including the Middle East, Africa, China, and North and South America.

Soil loss on farms is a serious problem that can be difficult to fix. The rich soil of a productive farm may have taken 10,000 years or more to form!

WORDS TO KNOW

agriculture the cultivation of plants and animals for food.

biodiversity the variety of plant and animal life in a particular habitat.

canal an artificial waterway constructed to allow the passage of boats inland.

deforestation the action of clearing a wide area of trees.

drought a long period of low rainfall, leading to a shortage of water.

energy power to provide light and heat or to run machines.

environment the surroundings in which an animal or plant lives.

extinction when every member of a species (kind) of living thing has died out.

fossil fuels natural fuels such as coal or gas formed millions of years ago from the remains of living plants or animals.

freight goods transported by truck, train, ship, or aircraft.

geologist a scientist who studies the rocks, minerals, and processes that make up Earth.

greenhouse effect the trapping of the sun's warmth in Earth's atmosphere due to the release of such gases as carbon dioxide.

hydroelectric power energy that comes from flowing water driving a turbine.

irrigate to supply water to crops.

mechanical energy the energy possessed by an object, such as a wind turbine, because of its motion.

mining digging under the earth for rocks and minerals.

natural resources materials or substances found in nature that people extract because they are useful.

ore the material from which a valuable mineral can be extracted.

piers tall, vertical structures designed to support bridges.

tectonic plates the massive plates that make up Earth's crust.

telecommunication communication over a distance by cable, telephone, and radio signals.

terrace a section of land resembling steps made flat by cutting into the side of a hill or mountain.

topography the arrangement of physical features in a landscape.

trawler a fishing boat that drags a wide-mouthed net along the bottom of the ocean to catch fish.

turbine a machine for producing power, in which a wheel or rotor is made to revolve by a fast-moving flow of air, gas, or water.

urbanization the process of making an area more urban (like a town or city).